CROSSING FORBIDDEN BOUNDARIES

The Grace Tabernacle Story

Gary Washburn

Acknowledgments

First and foremost thank you Jesus! You are the great author and finisher of my faith. Thank you, Pam for being my wife, my friend, my lover and my wise counselor, as well as a good editor. Thank you to my children, Sarah and Andrew, for growing up in a pastor's home when you had rather your father be anything else than a pastor. I know it was not always easy on you. Thank you, Mom for always believing in me and encouraging me to do my best. Thank you, Ken for being such a good son in law and father to my six precious grandchildren; Moriah, Julia, Anna, Jackson, Grant, and Timothy David. Thank you to Larry and Terry Zolnowski and my six adopted grandchildren; Brooke, John, Josh, Jessica, Luke and Grace.

Thank you, Larry and Charlotte Meeks, and Tony and Joan Defoe for being the fun friends that we need. You always help us to learn to laugh again when we need to lighten up.

Thank you to Carlton and Dorothy Baker, Rick and Elizabeth Palmer, and Larry and Charlotte Meeks. You are dear friends as well as my church elders who have faithfully stood by my side and given me wise counsel and encouragement for every area of my life. Thank you to Danny and Marybeth Harvey who took a bold stand with me when it was not easy to do.

Thanks to my wonderful church staff and families that make church an exciting place to be. You guys are the greatest! Thank you, Terry and Kathi Wilkinson, John and Christina Kimer, David and Julie Ayris, Brian and Jenni Highberger. Thank you, Jenni for patiently formatting this book.

Special thanks to Sherry Wilson for editing this manuscript and encouraging me to become a writer. Finally, thank you to everyone at Grace Tabernacle. You have laughed at my silly sense of humor and encouraged me to keep preaching long after I should have stopped! Together this is our story.

"You yourselves are our letter, written on our hearts, known and read by everybody" 2 Cor. 3:2

Endorsements

"Of the writing of books there is no end. When I look for a book the first thing I consider is the author. Is he just writing, or is he speaking and writing out of life and LIFE ETERNAL. I have known Gary for a long time he is writing out of life and the life of Jesus, so his writings have life. All that has life like this is very helpful and motivating. This will bless you."

Peter Lord
Author/Speaker
Retired Pastor of Park Avenue Baptist Church in Titusville, Florida

"Gary Washburn has laid it all out there in Crossing Forbidden Boundaries. You'll learn from the successes as well as the failures. What I love about Pastor Gary and Grace Tabernacle is that they don't sugarcoat the gospel or pretend that everything is perfect, but they have built an authentic church seeking after the heart of God. We need more churches like this in the days we live in. Prepare to have your paradigm rocked as you are challenged and changed by Crossing Forbidden Boundaries."

John Bevere
Author/Speaker
Messenger International
Colorado Springs/ Australia/ United Kingdom

"There is surely no book of this nature on the market today that is more enlightening to expose the hurt in Church life with a healthy, loving and yet, bare-knuckled approach to show the rich benefits of proper response to problems. Yes, there is life after church splits and problems, abundant life! Reading this book will serve to comfort the hurting as well as steer some through the minefields of relationships without serious injury. This is a map showing the way through trouble to triumph.

Jack Taylor
Dimensions Ministries
Melbourne, Florida

Table of Contents

Chapter 1

A Whole Lot Of Shaking Going On!

As the piano and organ music played, a short and pudgy, middle aged woman slowly made her way to the altar and stood directly in front of me. Her face revealed a heavily burdened heart inside. She was one of my best Sunday school teachers and a dedicated Christian lady. It was not uncommon for her to come to the church altar for prayer. I asked for some women from our congregation to come and pray for her. As eight women gathered around her and began to pray, she fell to her knees and cried, sobbing deeply. Her face and neck broke out in drops of sweat as her body shook. I extended the altar call to the rest of the congregation purposely trying to avoid drawing attention to this woman. But her crying grew louder and louder, and it interrupted my concentration.

There was something so unusual about the sound of her cries. It was as if she was being tormented by something from within. Finally, I could not

> *"Are you in torment?" I asked. Without hesitation she answered, "Yes! Yes! I am in torment!"*

ignore her loud cries any longer. I was surprised to hear what came out of my mouth next. "Are you in torment?" I asked. Without hesitation she answered, "Yes! Yes! I am in torment!" At that moment, I knew I was in over my head. Where was the evangelist when I needed him? I didn't know what to do next.

This had all started when a youth evangelist came to our church. It was already day ten of what was originally to be a four-day youth revival. Our traditional church was experiencing a very untraditional revival, unmistakably by the hand of God!

The youth evangelist's thinning hair revealed he was older than he looked. His flamboyant style seemed to amuse everyone. Each night he strutted like a peacock across the platform wearing a different flashy colored suit and matching shoes that equaled his colorful and outgoing personality. The accessories of gold jewelry added to the flare.

It was obvious that beyond the glitz and showmanship, there was an anointing of God on this youth evangelist. The evidence of people encountering the power of God each night was undeniable. His confident and charismatic style created quite a stir around town and drew crowds of people to our church revival. Without fail, every night at the end of his sermon, people would flock to the altar for salvation or repentance of some sin. I was astonished to see such a response among our church people, as well as people in our community who had never attended our church. This was a real revival unlike anything I had ever seen before.

Each night he asked the congregation to allow God to show them what needed to be cleansed or removed from their homes. And each night people returned with large garbage bags full of items to discard. There were music

CD's, videos, magazines; many were blatantly Satanic or demonic, while others appeared slightly evil. There were witchcraft items, pentagram jewelry, pornography, and tarot cards. Some teens brought their gang emblems and colors. Others brought packs of cigarettes and chewing tobacco.

Many shared how God told them specifically what items to clean out of their lives and bring to the church in repentance. The church platform was beginning to look more like a garbage dump. Everyone had something that they were willing to remove from their life. The word had spread throughout the town that a real revival was occurring in our little church. People within the community and from other churches eagerly came to see what God was doing.

On Tuesday night of the second week, our traditional church observed something we had never seen before. After the evangelist concluded his message, he quietly walked over to me. He whispered in my ear, "I feel sick; you close out the service however you are led." His words caught me off guard but I proceeded to give an altar call, while he left the building.

Little did I know that the next few minutes would become life changing for me as well as many others who were present. This was the moment the Sunday School teacher came forward for prayer and cried out that she was in torment. After the ladies prayed for her, I joined in and prayed for her to have peace. That is when things got even worse. Suddenly, her face began to change. Her neck and face turned blood red and the veins in her neck began to bulge. Through gritted teeth, she started growling like a mean dog. I knew I was seeing something that was not human. I had read about similar experiences, but had always been skeptical since I had never seen it for myself. I knew I had to do something quickly. I shot up a silent flare prayer. "God help me now," I prayed under my breath.

Her body was trembling violently, and blood began to drip from her nose onto her chin. At the same time, I felt sweat running down my legs. I was afraid, but I knew there was no turning back! I reached forward and laid my hands on her head. The sound of authority in my voice surprised me. "Satan, I bind you and all your demons in this woman and in this atmosphere in the name and through the blood of Jesus. I command you to come out of her and do not return!"

After this I led her to pray with me. Whenever I led her to repeat the words, "the blood of Jesus" she would choked up and not be able to say "the blood of Jesus". This demon was in some strange way restraining her from saying the words about the blood of Jesus. So now I spoke to the demon and demanded that it release her because of the authority of the blood of Jesus. Finally, this time she repeated after me the phrase "the blood of Jesus". Instantly, her face and shoulders relaxed as if something was loosed from her.

> *This demon was in some strange way restraining her from saying the words about the blood of Jesus.*

After repeating these words, she spontaneously spurted out a stream of words that sounded like a foreign language. She lifted her hands and began to shout loud praises thanking God for setting her free from torment. The congregation watched with amazement and then joined in with shouts of "Hallelujah" and hand clapping. I was just as surprised as anyone.

The atmosphere in the sanctuary changed instantly. Fear and tension evaporated as the peace of God invaded the room, much like the calm after a storm. Later, many in the congregation reported experiencing the sensation of peace, as if a cool heavenly breeze had brushed over them. I continued to stand before the congregation feeling numb and in awe, while marveling at what had just occurred. It seemed like a dream or a movie. I was thinking that I would never forget this life-defining moment. Drained emotionally, and feeling weak in the knees, I sat down pondering over and

> **Shaking always precedes awakening!**

over again every detail of what had just happened. I assumed the church service was over, but no one wanted to go home.

It was an awkward moment when no one knew what to do next. Finally, a deacon in our church named David, hugged me and asked permission to speak to the church. I gladly surrendered the microphone. He spoke to the congregation saying, "I would not have believed this had I not seen it with my own eyes. I knew there had to be more to the Christian life than what I was experiencing! I was considering going to another church, but tonight, God showed me that He is right here. I know I need to stay here and support this pastor." Showing their agreement, the congregation broke out in cheers and applause.

Not long after this, it was David who came to me feeling led of God to start a deliverance ministry in our church. Now that our eyes had been opened to the realm of the demonic I knew this was a much needed ministry. David began the deliverance ministry in a small room dedicated for prayer. At first we named the deliverance ministry 'prayer counseling' because most of our members did not have a clue as to what deliverance was. We did not publicize that we started a deliverance ministry to cast out demons. However, it wasn't long before people all around our area were coming to David for deliverance. The news about our church casting out demons spread like wildfire, and this caused more people to attend our church.

Our traditional church, being shaken by the power of God, was the key that unlocked the door to our great spiritual awakening. This experience quickly became public knowledge throughout our community. The fact that I had publicly cast a demon out of a Christian lady, who also spoke in tongues, was crossing a forbidden boundary within my own denomination. I was wondering how the leaders in my church and denomination would respond. I was about to find out.

I began studying the scriptures more about this subject of casting out demons. I was surprised to discover that casting out demons marked about one third of Jesus' ministry. In John 14:12 Jesus said, *"Truly, truly I say to you, he who believes in Me, the works I do he shall do also..."* It was clear that demons were real and many of the problems that people have can be attributed to demons.

A new awareness of the power of God began after this incredible encounter with a demon at church.

At first I was quite surprised to see a positive reaction from our traditional congregation. It was becoming obvious to me that there had been an underlying hunger in the people for such manifestations of the power of the Holy Spirit. Almost immediately, the church began to grow in number as people searching to experience more of the power of God found a church home with us. With the increase of spiritually hungry people came more freedom in worship expressions. People felt free to lift their hands and shout "Hallelujah" during the church service.

As attendance increased, so did our church income. Before this power encounter, we had always struggled to meet our church budget, but that changed dramatically. People became excited about giving. Some told me they couldn't wait until it was offering time! The church's mortgage, which previously seemed impossible to pay off, was paid off faster than anyone expected.

Our dramatic shaking had a lasting effect. Though the nightly revival meetings only lasted three and a half weeks, the church's awakening continued for several years. In some of us, it still continues today. But for others, this had already gone too far, and something needed to be done about it! More shaking was about to happen. This was only the beginning.

Chapter 2

Not Everyone Wants Revival

By now our church had two services on Sunday morning. This was not because we had an overflow of people, but rather to appease those who wanted a more traditional service. The 8:00 A.M. traditional service decreased in attendance, while the 10:30 A.M. contemporary service attendance increased. (I have since learned it is not a good thing to have two different types of services for people. It only causes more division rather than unity.)

During the contemporary service, we experienced a new freedom. Sometimes the service would continue for two hours without any preaching, just worship and testimonies. Someone would spontaneously start singing a hymn or praise song and everyone would join in.

Many used this new found freedom to give impromptu testimonies of how God was changing their lives. After a testimony, the congregation would break out in supportive applause and amen's of agreement. We were learning how to let the Holy Spirit lead the church service rather than following our routine way of church. It was refreshing to be released from the expected way of doing things.

> *We were learning how to let Holy Spirit lead the church service rather than following our routine way of church.*

Not knowing what was going to happen next was risky, but at the same time exhilarating.

According to a Barna poll, only seven percent of the churches in my denomination were classified as charismatic by their pastors. I believed God was moving our church in that direction, or at least to be open minded enough to realize He had so much more for us to experience.

With this new freedom, I felt God would have me restudy the gifts of the Spirit, this time letting the Holy Spirit be my teacher. I threw out my old notes that I had compiled from studying various commentaries. I asked God to teach me as if I had never heard or read about spiritual gifts. (I think God was waiting for me to ask for this.) As He opened my eyes during my personal study, I developed a new understanding, which I began sharing with my congregation on Wednesday nights.

My perspective was changing from the one I held seven years earlier when I first became the pastor of this church. At that time, I mocked charismatics! I believed they were lunatics! I believed those who claimed to speak in tongues were parroting what they had heard from people that I nicknamed charis-maniacs.

But now my new understanding reflected the fact that God was changing me. I had to repent for mocking charismatics. I had been blind but now I was beginning to see. I had received the Baptism of the Holy Spirit and was privately praying in tongues. I still had a lot of questions about the gifts and this study was born out of my own personal desire for revelation. My school of the Holy Spirit would be from on the job training. I was not sure how my congregation would react since my denomination did not welcome the manifestation of these gifts.

This revival brought along many of the gifts of the Holy Spirit that our church had never experienced before. By now our congregation had been exposed to the gift of tongues, deliverance, as well as people falling under the power of the Holy Spirit. But the big question that remained was, how would my congregation respond to my changing theology? I heard someone say, "God never contradicts His Word, but He

> *"God never contradicts His Word, but He often contradicts my understanding of His Word".*

often contradicts my understanding of His Word". This statement best describes the way I felt God was teaching me. It was like He was taking me back to the beginning of everything I knew about His Word and re-teaching me all over again. There were so many things I needed to unlearn in order to be able to receive the truth.

All of these new manifestations of the power of God in our church were visible and undeniable. Changes in people's lives and in our church services were obvious. All this came about when God shook our church alive to the power of the Holy Spirit.

Forbid not speaking in tongues!

I knew the time would come when I would have to take a stand for my new beliefs, but I did not think it would come so soon. One Wednesday night, I was teaching about the gift of tongues. Using the scriptures to support my position, I stepped out of my comfort zone and declared tongues as a valid and current spiritual gift. This was crossing a forbidden boundary in my churches denominational doctrine.

What I was declaring would upset some, and at the same time, liberate others. As I looked at the faces of my congregation, I was surprised that no one appeared shocked by my statement. Did they hear me? I decided to take one more step by sharing the fact that I personally prayed in tongues in my private prayer time. I encouraged people to ask the Holy Spirit to guide them and then to be open to praying in tongues in their private time with God. Again, my eyes scanned the faces of my congregation; I found no evidence of alarm. I was excited and relieved that I could be so open and transparent without opposition.

In the days following this service, many told me that this teaching was new to them and that they wanted to know more. I was encouraged by their hunger for this new revelation. It was liberating to speak from my personal experience with God. I was no longer bound by the denominational teachings of my Bible College or peers. I was no longer intimidated by traditions that the majority of my denomination believed. I was taking a bold stand, and I felt good about it. No one was opposing me, at least no one apparent.

God Arranging Divine Connections

Across town, another shaking was taking place in another young minister's life. Terry had been asking God for more awareness of God's presence in his life. He and two other pastors from his church attended a Spirit-filled worship conference. At the end of the conference the three of them met in a vacant room to talk and pray about all they had just seen and heard. During this time of sharing and prayer is when he encountered an overwhelming awareness of God's presence. Terry was the worship leader at the contemporary service at his church. One of the other men was the leader of the traditional service. As the contemporary service grew in attendance, so did a spirit of competition between the two pastors. During this time of sharing and prayer, this issue of competition was dealt with. Terry and the other pastor forgave each other for the past and healing took place in their hearts. Terry began to cry uncontrollably for a long time, not realizing the depth of what was happening to him. This was not just a one time emotional experience. It was not until later that Terry realized it was the baptism of the Holy Spirit that he had experienced on that day. There was a new power in His life that was noticeable to anyone who knew Terry.

For ten years Terry served as worship leader in a large denominational church. When he returned from this conference people began to comment that he was different. With a greater boldness, he encouraged people to express their worship to God freely, openly, and without the fear of man. He had a deeper passion to lead people into greater intimacy with God. As a result, he saw a different response to the worship during the contemporary service. Pouring out their hearts openly before the Lord, people filled the altar with weeping and prayer, and some even spoke in tongues. He was encouraging the people to be expressive in whatever ways they felt the Holy Spirit was leading them. This opened the door for freedom like never before in this traditional church. The manifest presence of God during worship was undeniable.

Church attendance in the contemporary service surpassed the attendance in the traditional televised service, however, not everyone was as pleased about it as Terry. The church leadership was not in agreement with this new found freedom in worship and demanded Terry to "tone it down" and confine worship to a strict time limit. This appeared to be an ultimatum.

Some members of my church knew Terry and the frustrations he was feeling. They urged him to meet with me, since our church was transitioning from a traditional church to a more charismatic style. As we met, he openly shared about his recent encounter with God at the worship conference.

As I listened, it was obvious that God had opened Terry's spiritual eyes and ears to a new understanding of what it means to worship God freely. He had a new way of thinking. He knew God had more for him than what he had traditionally been taught. He was hungry to see his church experience more of what God wanted for them, but he was not convinced that his church would allow it.

At the close of our conversation, Terry confided that he believed we would be ministering together someday. I remember smiling and thinking to myself, "That's nice, but I doubt it". As I leaned back in my chair, I said, "Terry, I am content to spend the rest of my life ministering in this little denominational church. I have a freedom here that I have never had before!" I told him that I recently taught about the gifts of the Holy Spirit and confessed to the congregation that I spoke in tongues and everyone seemed open to all I was teaching. He was surprised that I was able to be so open and transparent in such a traditional church. I saw a longing in Terry's eyes for the same type of freedom.

Another Divine Connection

One evening while making visits at the local hospital, I met John at the visitor information desk. I recognized his face but I could not remember his name. So I introduced myself to him and discovered he was the youth minister and worship leader at another traditional church in our same area. Like me, he was at the hospital visiting some church members. As we struck up a casual conversation, I could tell that there was something I liked about this young man. His personality came across to me as bold but at the same time caring. He was young but I sensed he was wise beyond his years. I liked him instantly.

Since my church was looking for a youth minister, I mentioned this to him and asked if he would submit a resume, and he agreed. A few weeks later, our church youth committee and I interviewed John and unanimously agreed to offer him the position.

The next day I called him to let him know the youth minister position was his if he still wanted it. During our conversation John confessed that something didn't feel right about the timing. He said that he did believe we would be working together one day. I thought to myself, where had I heard that one before! This was beginning to feel really weird. Was it possible that somehow God would put all three of us together one day in the same church? But how?

Storms Approaching

Little did I know, a storm was blowing in. Behind closed doors, my associate pastor and several deacons held a series of secret meetings to determine how to remove me as pastor. Together they concluded that I was crossing forbidden boundaries and was teaching false doctrine. I had no idea that any of this was happening. Together, they drafted a letter that would be eventually sent to every church member. This letter warned them of a "charismatic takeover" by their pastor and advising them to demand my resignation in order to save "their church." They would wait for just the right time to make their move.

Though I did not know it at the time, my meetings with Terry and John were not coincidental, but were divinely orchestrated. God's hand was positioning me for the coming storm. But first, there was a question that I would be forced to answer.

> *God's hand was positioning me for the coming storm.*

cᐯo

Chapter 3

The Question You Need
To Ask Your Church

"Who's in control?"

One night, in a lengthy deacon's meeting, we were at a standstill. A decision was needed over a trivial issue. Exasperated, the deacon to my right looked me in the eye and said, "Who's in charge in this church?" Puzzled by this question, I hesitated before responding with what I thought was the obvious answer, "God is in charge." Not satisfied, the deacon leaned forward, pointed his finger in my face, and repeated slower and louder, "Who makes the final decision in matters concerning the church?"

> *"Who makes the final decision in matters concerning the church?"*

Now I was getting flustered because I knew that he knew the answer, but I clarified the process for him anyway. "After the pastor and deacons or a committee brings issues to the church business meeting, the congregation votes on the matter."

Satisfied with my answer, he sat back in his chair, and smiled as he said, "That is my point. God calls a shepherd to lead His sheep not deacons, not committees, not congregational consensus. Either you are God's shepherd and are in charge of leading this flock, or you are nothing more than a hireling!"

The room became awkwardly silent. I knew we were all tired and maybe getting a little irritable, but this sounded like a personal attack. No one, including me, knew what to say next. Did this deacon, who I thought was my friend, just insult me? Did he just call me a hireling? Did he not remember our church budget?

My pastoral salary was close to the poverty level. My family lived in a small pastorium that was in dire need of repair. Our family car was a ten-year-old worn-out minivan. The church provided me with a dilapidated used car for ministry. As I drove it down the street, billows of smoke left a cloudy trail behind, causing some to mistake my car for a mosquito-spraying vehicle. My kids were mortified when I drove them to school in it. Anyone with a brain could see that I was not serving as pastor for the money or the benefits.

What was the point that this deacon was trying to make? Was he pointing out a fatal flaw in our church's government? Was our decision-making process not in line with the way God intended His church to operate? "Who's in charge?" was a very valid question prompting me to take a closer look at the way our church was governed.

I hated church business meetings.

My only pastoral experience was in congregationally governed churches, where the foundation of the church government was a constitution and bylaws. In this form of government, an issue could be introduced at a business meeting and then the congregation voted on everything from budgets to bulletins. Usually these business meetings were held monthly or quarterly in place of a Wednesday night prayer meeting.

I observed that most members stayed home on business meeting night due to lack of interest. I wanted to as well, but as the Pastor, I had to moderate the business meeting. It was obvious that the real majority of members were voting with their feet not to attend church business meetings. By choice, the majority of the church members never attended a single business meeting. The few who made the pilgrimage became the majority and ruled the church through voting. As shepherd of this flock, I was at the mercy of this small and vocal majority.

Church Ruled By The People

For twenty years I had noticed an unhealthy cycle in the churches that I had pastored. Without fail every two years there would be an issue that would surface during the business meeting that would eventually cause major conflict in the church. This conflict resulted in losing much-needed members for our struggling church. I could sense when it was about time for something like this to happen. My stomach would get upset and I would feel anxious for no apparent reason, and then division would hit our church again, just like it was hurricane season. I felt helpless. All I knew to do was batten down the hatches and endure the storm. I could not understand why this cycle happened like clockwork every two years.

The history of my current church revealed another unhealthy cycle. Every two or three years they would hire a new pastor. I had to wonder what happened to cause a pastor to leave a church after only two years. It would take at least two years to get to know your people. This was suspicious and certainly not healthy for a church or a pastor. By this time I had been the pastor of this church for seven years. I was beginning to realize why this church was experiencing so many opportunities for a church split.

Please understand my intent is not to criticize those in congregationally-ruled churches, but to point out how this form of church government undermines a pastor from ever becoming the leader God has called him to become. It becomes impossible to lead if you are not given the authority to lead and make all final decisions. The authority in a congregational government stays within the congregation. Therefore, the congregation leads and the pastor

> *This form of church government undermines a pastor from ever becoming the leader God has called him to become.*

follows their directives. Without realizing it, a hireling is born.

In my experience I observed that the democratic form of government can erode into a power struggle among the members, as well as between the pastor and the members. The members feel that they have just as much authority as the pastor. In fact they may feel that they have more authority because they have a majority of members willing to vote their way on any given issue. Get enough members to vote your way and you can change anything or do anything you desire in a congregationally governed church. I find it inconceivable that people could join a church today and have the authority to fire a pastor tomorrow, but it could happen. God never intended churches to be governed by a popular vote. There has to be a better way!

When a church has a new pastor every two years or

Who is the church boss?

so, it is nearly impossible for a pastor to become the leader in the eyes of the members. In a church governed by the people, eventually someone with a controlling spirit will assume the position of "church boss." The church boss is an unofficial position, usually attained by tenure and intimidation. The church boss could be either male or female. The church boss could be self-appointed or appointed by a group seeking an articulate person as their spokesperson. Usually, the biggest mouth or the biggest pocketbook gets to be church boss. The pastor will eventually have a show down with him or her. No church is big enough for the both of them.

To reveal the identity of the church boss, tip over one of his sacred cows - suggest change! The church boss will quickly challenge you with, "We've never done it that way before" or "That is not the way we do it!"

If you have not encountered similar church politics, thank the Lord for sparing you the heartache! The pastor, with an unofficial church boss in his church, might resemble a city manager who has to carry out the wishes of the voters in order to keep his job! The pastor can still have influence, but only to the extent that the church boss and his cronies agree with him. It's a delicate situation to be in, especially in smaller churches. The smaller the church, the more influential the church boss becomes.

As long as the pastor and the church boss agree, there is harmony within the church. When the pastor bucks him, he turns into the "church bully boss". This is witch-craft in action within the church! It is blatant rebellion against the pastor's God- ordained authority. Surprisingly, the church bully boss believes he is driven by justice and fairness. He believes he is going to save the church from a pastor gone wild!

If we knew the history of this church boss, we would probably discover there were a series of pastors with whom he had butted heads and run out of town. It is likely that each time a pastor left the church, the same group was having a problem with his leadership.

Are you are in a church where you frequently have a new pastor? If you are, you might want to ask, "Who is really in control of my church?"

> *Are you are in a church where you frequently have a new pastor?*

The Church Committees

Within the animal kingdom a grouping of whales is called a pod, a grouping of cows, a herd, a grouping of wolves, a pack; but a grouping of buzzards is called a committee! Maybe this is why I felt like I was dying when I attended those long, boring, committee meetings. In some of these meetings I felt like the buzzards were circling over the church expecting to eat another pastor's carcass.

In our church, committees were nothing more than miniature church business meetings where the majority ruled. Here again the pastor's role as leader was undermined by a majority vote by the committee members. The pastor could attend any committee meeting and have influence, but in most cases had no vote in the final vote of the committee itself. The majority ruled!

Many church members in the United States believe our country's democratic form of government is an acceptable means of governing the church. They think that the majority voting in agreement is the sign that God has spoken. Agreement does not mean they have heard the voice of the Lord.

God delights in guiding His church with supernatural direction. He expects us to pray and seek His will and wait until He leads us. Has church voting replaced the need for supernatural gifts and guidance? Does God wait until we vote before He acts?

God's government is a kingdom, not a democracy. God placed a pastor to shepherd His sheep. We, the sheep, are to recognize the Great Shepherd's voice through

> *God's government is a kingdom, not a democracy.*

our pastor, and submit to our pastor's leadership.

Isn't this risky to place so much power upon one man? Yes. But don't think it takes any less risk to put that same power upon a group of people. Actually, this is a burden no one man can carry alone. God will give him the gifts of like-minded people to assist him in fulfilling his calling.

The Gift Of Elders

"Then the LORD said to Moses, 'Summon before me seventy of the leaders of Israel. Bring them to the Tabernacle to stand there with you. 17 I will come down and talk to you there. I will take

some of the Spirit that is upon you, and I will put the Spirit upon them also. They will bear the burden of the people along with you, so you will not have to carry it alone.'" Numbers 11:16-17.

By spending the majority of his time with God, with the Word, and in prayer, the pastor can maintain a heart after God. Elders multiply the effectiveness of a pastor by assuming administrative and leadership responsibilities and by advising the pastor in making decisions. Elders are not the pastor's "yes" men. They advise and counsel the pastor using the wisdom God has given them. They are to be spiritual fathers to the people having the same spirit that the pastor has upon his life. There is no room for power-hungry egos in God's church leadership. Church government is only as good as it follows the leading of the Holy Spirit. In the end the final decision in all matters must remain the responsibility of the pastor alone. The buck stops with him!

There is no perfect church on earth. With this understanding in mind, we need to walk in love, having grace and mercy toward leadership that will make mistakes from time to time. Leaders learn how to lead

> **If it's unanimous, it must be God, right?**

from trial and error. Risk taking is part of leading. A pastor cannot base his decisions upon the consensus of opinions. People must trust the heart of their shepherd rather than wait for a majority vote to assume God's leading.

On one occasion, Israel's elders unanimously agreed upon a battle strategy that they presumed would bring certain victory over an opposing Philistine army. The result was a humiliating disaster for God's people

(I Samuel 4:3-10). Though these elders reached a unanimous decision, they had not heard from God.

> *We should never assume that unity is a sign that God has spoken.*

We should never assume that unity is a sign that God has spoken. The goal of all leadership is to hear from God. Does this prompt you to ask, "Who has God placed in charge of leading my church?"

It prompted me to re-examine the church government that I had been a part of my entire ministry. I uncovered the reality that congregational government was cutting off the head that God designed to lead His church. Though God called me to lead, I was not leading. The power to lead was in the hands of the people. Was I nothing more than a hireling? I needed the truth! Little did I know that something was about to happen that would reveal who was really in control of this church!

Chapter 4

The Ugly Side Of Church

Disgruntled, my assistant pastor found a group of like-minded deacons with whom to share his growing frustrations about my changing doctrinal beliefs. Storm clouds gathered strength as this newly formed group held secret, unofficial meetings.

These dissatisfied deacons had sought the counsel of both local and state denominational leaders without my knowledge. They expressed concerns about a "charismatic takeover" by their pastor. These denominational leaders must have agreed that a plan of action was necessary.

However, neither the local nor the state denominational representatives ever contacted me to indicate that they were aware of a problem, not even as much as a courtesy call! I thought this was underhanded, as I had faithfully served in this denomination for almost 20 years.

In an "unofficial" meeting, the assistant pastor and some deacons drafted a letter. Feeling the need for urgency, they warned the congregation of my dangerous doctrines and my attempt to take over their church. In this letter they called upon the membership to demand my resignation immediately so the members could have "their church" back. The deacons and my assistant pastor signed the warning letter that was mailed to every member of our congregation without my knowledge.

We held our regularly monthly deacons meeting on Sunday evening. I sensed something did not feel right but I was not sure what it was. During this meeting, I looked each deacon in the eye and asked him if there were any issues or problems we needed to discuss. The room was silent.

The deacons who had signed the letter wore plastic smiles, as if to say, "Everything is under control." They knew the letter to the congregation was already in the mail. I imagine that in their own minds, they thought things were finally getting under control, as long as it was under their control. I had no clue that this strange feeling I was having was the calm before the storm.

On Monday, people started receiving the letter in the mail. The phone started ringing off the hook. Some members called me, asking what the letter was all about. One person read the letter to me over the phone. At first, I thought that this must have been some kind of joke, until I heard the names of the men who had signed it. Suddenly, I realized that I had been betrayed by a Judas.

My heart sank. Why was all this done behind my back? Why all the deception? I was shocked. This felt like a stab in my heart. Something had to be done quickly.

I called for an emergency deacons meeting for that night. I needed to meet with all of the deacons, especially those who had signed this letter demanding my resignation. There were more deacons that stood with me than against me. Those deacons standing with me were just as shocked as I was about the letter.

Yesterday, these deacons expressed that there were no problems with the direction of our church. Today the truth was finally surfacing. The most painful part of this was the deception from people I considered my friends. I identified with the way David must have felt when he wrote: *"It is not an enemy who taunts me— I could bear that. It is not my foes who so arrogantly insult me— I could have hidden from them. Instead, it is you—my equal, my companion and close friend. What good fellowship we enjoyed as we walked together to the house of God." Psalm 55:12-13*

This breach of trust severed friendships. For several years we had weathered some difficult storms together and each time we had resolved differences and moved forward. This time was different. I worried, would the progress the church had made during these last few years be lost? Couldn't these deacons see the ways God was blessing our church?

Our church was growing and was finally out of debt! Since the youth revival, our church atmosphere was fresh and exciting. People freely expressed themselves in praise and worship. As for me, I felt freer than at any other time in my life as a pastor! Now all this freedom was being threatened to be taken away. Was this new found freedom worth fighting for?

Had I been naïve to think such spiritual progress would go unopposed? There had been some resistance along the way but nothing as ugly as this uprising. Tempers were beginning to flare up and a line had been drawn down the middle of the church. A spiritual civil war had begun.

It sickened me to imagine what might happen as I anticipated the outcome. This issue would be settled on the battlefield, the church business meeting. Those behind the letter-writing campaign would attempt to rally voters for their cause - to vote me out as pastor. Knowing it would be ugly, I was not looking forward to the next business meeting which was soon about to happen.

A confrontation was inevitable in a church, governed by the people and for the people. The pastor had no more authority than the newest church member did when it all came down to a vote. It was all a matter of politics: get other members to support your opinion, to vote your way, then the majority ruled! Surely, this wasn't the way God intended us to lead His church.

The enemy made sure the un-churched around town heard about our church war that was forming! Could this be why *"there are twenty-three million born-again Christians in the United States who refuse to go to church anymore"?* [1] Now, I could understand; some days, I didn't want to go to church, but I was the pastor! I had to remind myself that the people against me were not the enemy.

Many of the people who opposed me were just doing what they thought was right. Some tried to remain neutral and not take sides. Some had an agenda and knew exactly what they were doing. Their controlling, religious spirits had intimidated previous pastors, and they were resorting to similar tactics.

This was a spiritual battle, and though the enemy was invisible, the people he used were very visible and vocal. I found it tough to separate the enemy from the people he used. My emotions got involved, and it became personal to me.

At first I hoped that we could get along even though we disagreed on "minor" doctrinal issues. However, the issues I thought were minor were major in their eyes. So,

I hoped that our love for each other was strong enough to keep us united and work through our disagreements. It was Martin Luther who said, "In essentials unity, in nonessentials liberty, in all things charity." It soon

> *"In essentials unity, in non-essentials liberty, in all things charity."*

became apparent that as much as I wanted this, it was not happening here!

I believed that almost ten years as pastor of this church provided me enough supportive people to win this battle if it came down to a vote. I knew though, that behind the scenes, this was a vicious attack of the enemy to stop the progress that this church was making. The enemy was determined not to let this continue. Though I had been through previous church conflicts, nothing compared to this one.

By now I had been pastor of this church for almost ten years, which is longer than any pastor they had ever had. I wasn't planning on going anywhere. This was getting ugly but I was determined to endure it and keep moving the church forward. Surely, God would fight for me just as He had before…or would He?

Chapter 5

The Test Of Silence

What do you do when you don't know what to do and God is silent? It's a tough place to be but this is where I was.

I was in agony over the division in our church. I could not believe that what was happening was really happening. Desperately I prayed, "Father God, please speak to me. Tell me what to do to fix this broken church?" I didn't see or hear anything that I could recognize was God speaking to me. This was puzzling. Why would God be silent when I was in despair and I was desperately crying out to hear from Him? Was I wrong? Was He angry with me? Was this why He was not communicating to me?

I began questioning myself. "Was I wrong about the way I was leading the church? Was God angry at me for being too transparent with my congregation? Was this simply the enemy attacking me and the church?" I had to know the answers to these questions.

I wasn't expecting an audible voice, although that would have been nice. However, I did expect to receive some sense of God's direction in some way. I could always sense when God was showing me something. But this time, God seemed strangely quiet.

Sometimes when I read my Bible, the Holy Spirit seems to highlight a scripture as if He is saying to me, "Read this or pay attention to this". Other times, I recognize God's leading through a natural set of circumstances. By this time, I tried everything I knew to connect with God and yet I felt totally alone in my Gethsemane. I cried, I poured my heart out, I confessed every sin that came to my mind, rebuked every demon I knew to rebuke and still there was no indication that God was present, only deafening silence.

Could it be that God expected me to know the answer? As a parent, there were times when I didn't respond to my children's questions hoping that my lack of response was understood as the answer! Was this one of those times? I remembered from school that during a test the teacher does not talk. Could this be a test for me from God?

God already knew what was in my heart. Was the test for me to discover the depth of my faith? When I made decisions, would I walk by faith in God's word or would I cave in to the security of what I could see or touch? Did I really trust God?

Don't panic, stay calm, God is watching you, I would remind myself. The ultimate goal was to have a faith exactly like Jesus who was panic proof during the middle of a storm. He knew that this surprise uprising of people against me was going to happen, and He purposely chose not to stop it.

If only I had recognized this silent alarm from the Holy Spirit: "This is a test. It is only a test. This is a test of the Eternal Broadcasting System. If this had been an actual emergency you would have been directed to the nearest shelter of the Almighty." Part of the reason that

I did not recognize this as a test from God was that I was angry over the juvenile way that some of the leaders in our church were acting out.

This is a test. It is only a test. This is a test of the Eternal Broadcasting System.

Heck yeah I was angry!

To make matters worse I heard that one of the deacons was spreading some ugly remarks about my daughter who got pregnant before marriage. Even though she and her husband confessed their sin publicly and asked forgiveness from the church, this issue was being used to help build a case against me. I considered this a personal attack. This had nothing to do with the issues of change at our church. I was already angry and depressed and now to hear this made me even angrier.

The pressure was still accumulating. I felt like a walking time bomb, and I was dangerously close to exploding! People were trying to get me fired and now some were personally attacking my family.

I knew the Bible said to *"live peaceably with all men as much as lieth in you."* I told myself that I did that and had run out of peace a long time ago. I had prayed all I knew to pray but my prayers seemed to be ignored. I had cried out to God to help me deal with these difficult people, but nothing seemed to change. In error, I decided that God was not defending my family because He expected me to come to their defense. This was a big mistake!

Emotionally, I perceived everything was becoming a personal attack against me and my family. I was becoming very defensive. At night I stayed awake replaying this man's remarks about my kids and began to smolder with anger. Finally, I decided that he must be confronted about running his mouth and I was the one to do it. I visualized strategically what I would say to him and when I would do it. My plan was to confront this deacon during the evening emergency deacon's meeting. If he admitted his slander toward my family and apologized, I would drop the issue. But if he denied it, then I was going to deck him!

I could see in my mind the scenario of what would happen. I would clobber the deacon. The other deacons would pull me off of him; he would have me arrested, and my wife, Pam, would bail me out of jail. The next day the headlines would read, "Fight breaks out at local church! Pastor in jail!" I could see my sad face plastered next to the story. I knew my loss of control would lead to the death of my ministry, but at that moment, I did not care. I was in a dangerous place!

The Silence Of God Was Broken

On the morning of our evening emergency deacon's meeting, I headed to the gym to work off some of my stress. I knew if I continued with my secret plan that I would most likely be in jail by evening. I told no one what I was thinking. My mind was made up and I knew I was crossing a forbidden boundary.

> *God is setting you up to be blessed...if you don't mess it up!*

Someone had given me a cassette tape of John Bevere preaching at the Brownsville revival. I had heard some of it the previous day while driving in the car. On this morning as soon as I turned on the car, the tape started where it left off the day before with John's voice yelling loudly, "God is setting you up to be blessed…if you don't mess it up!" There was a long pause and for a moment I thought the tape broke. I turned off the car. I began to feel God's presence again. It had been a long time but I knew I could feel God's obvious presence in the car with me. At this moment, the hardness of my heart started to break. God had just spoken to me through this taped sermon!

I sat there in my driveway stunned at the presence of God and unable to move while I pondered those words. Suddenly God's Spirit broke the silence with these almost audible words piercing my heart. "That word is for you. If you don't stop right now and take your hands off of this matter, I'll take my hands off of you!" I heard God talking to my heart clearer than I have ever heard Him.

I slumped over the steering wheel and burst into tears and deep sobs. One word from God and my heart melted like wax. One moment in His unmistakable presence slew me. Without any hesitation I repented out loud to God. "I am so sorry, Lord. I repent of my anger towards this man and all of the people with him. I repent of being angry with You. I repent of thinking such evil thoughts and I surrender to Your will, whatever that is. Have Your way, Lord." In a flash, the dam of hard feelings broke and the sudden flood of tears washed away my anger.

Immediately, I felt a cool breeze sweep like a circle through my heart and my body. This was a literal, physical, as well as spiritual sensation. It wasn't the cool air from the air conditioner blowing upon me, it was the

Holy Spirit blowing upon me. I knew in an instant that the Holy Spirit had swept through my soul and cleansed me of all of my malice. God had rescued me from myself. I was a different man from just a moment ago.

I ran back into the foyer of our house still sobbing and trembling from hearing the voice of God. I yelled out my wife's name and Pam heard the sobs in my voice and ran to meet me. Catching my breath between deep sobs I told Pam what had just happened. It was obvious to her that I had encountered God. Moments earlier she had kissed a hardened and sad man goodbye at the door. Now, she looked into the face of a broken man who had just heard and felt God. The difference was unmistakable.

I confessed to her what I had intended on doing during the deacons' meeting that night. Both of us prayed and re-surrendered our lives and put all of these circumstances into the hands of the Lord. A great part of the spirit of heaviness lifted at that moment of surrender. I still felt sadness over the condition of our church, but at least I was confident that God knew everything that was going on and He knew I was being treated unfairly. It was a test; it was only a test.

God was setting me up to be blessed, and my plan would have destroyed everything by retaliation. God did not need my justice to rectify any situation. He didn't need me to straighten anyone out! Instead, He was straightening me out.

"For thou prevents him with the blessings of goodness..." *Psalm 21:3.*

I believe God stepped in and prevented me from ruining His plan by trying to implement my plan.

He literally "prevented" me with His goodness.

Lessons I learned from God's silent times:

1. Don't misinterpret God's silence as His disapproval.

2. When God is silent, make your soul be still and rest in the fact that God is in charge.

"Be still and know that I am God." Psalm 46:10.

Looking back, I wish I had passed the test of silence without God having to stop me from taking matters into my own hands. When God was silent, I should have been silent. His mercy prevailed in spite of my immaturity. Now, whenever God is silent, I swear I can hear my conscience say,

"Remember, this is a test; it is only a test!"

Chapter 6

Leap Of Faith

The church atmosphere grew more intense by the minute. A church split appeared to be inevitable. This had become one of the lowest seasons in my life. On the phone, a friend of mine suggested, "Maybe you should just give them the baby." His words stung like a wasp. It wasn't what I wanted to hear, but it was what I needed to hear. Instantly, I knew again that God was talking to me this time through my friend. I became silent and listened as he continued.

He reminded me about King Solomon and two women who claimed the same baby as their own (I Kings 3:16-28). They stood before the king for him to decide the matter.

These women lived in one house, each having a baby the same age. One woman had switched the babies during the night after accidentally smothering her child when she laid on him during the night. When the other woman awakened to the dead baby at her side, she recognized that this baby was not her child.

The women argued back and forth before the king. "The living baby is my child; the dead one is yours." "No! You're lying. The dead baby is yours and the living one is mine!" The king shouted, "Guard, bring me a sword!" King Solomon told the women he would have the baby cut in two and give each woman half of the baby to settle the issue. The real mother of the living baby was shocked at the king's judgment. Her heart was breaking. She cried out, "No! Give her the baby; don't kill him."

King Solomon said, "The real mother has spoken!" The imposter was exposed with her own words, "Go ahead; divide the baby with the sword, let it be neither mine nor hers!" One woman was trying to save her child and the other woman was trying to save herself some personal pain. Personally, I believe Solomon never intended on killing the baby. His intent was to expose the real mother's heart from the imposter. The real mother would rather give up her child than have it murdered.

Like King Solomon, I was facing a dilemma. My situation was not as serious as killing a child, but swords had been drawn and sides taken over my leadership of the church. The baby was the church that I had pastored for the last nine years. This baby was soon to be divided by two opposing groups within the church. One group stood with me and God's new path for the church. The other group opposed this new direction and wanted the church to return to the way it had been – back to the comfortable, back to the traditional, back to everything being under their control.

It felt like if I were to resign as pastor, that I would be giving up "my baby". However, I was beginning to understand that God was telling me to let go. Why would God be telling me to resign as pastor?

My own insecurities began to surface. What would I do? I had been a pastor for most of my life; It was all I knew how to do! I did not have a back up plan for my life's work. Did God want me out of the ministry? I still had a mortgage and bills to pay. I had no reserves stashed away. I wanted details and assurances from God and He wanted me to trust Him with all of the details. These fears bombarded my mind, but I could still hear God in my heart saying, "Trust Me; give them the baby."

I could not figure out how my resignation could be God's will. Wasn't this giving up and giving in to the opposition? In the past, I would have I believed that I should stay and fight this out. After all, I had been there nine years. If it came down to a vote in a business meeting, I knew that I would have a majority of votes to keep me as pastor. At this point, I was crying out to God, asking Him to confirm His direction for me. I had to be sure that this was what God wanted me to do.

About an hour after this phone call, another friend called to try to encourage me and asked me to lunch. During our meal, he spoke words similar to those that my other friend had just spoken to me. I burst into tears knowing now that God was confirming everything I had heard just moments ago. He wanted me to let go and resign without having future plans. Like it or not, this was my personal test time.

This would not be easy. My kids had grown up in this church. My daughter had married here. In nine years, we witnessed dramatic changes for the better and invested our personal blood, sweat and tears. The best years of my ministry were here; at least, this is what I thought. I would have to let go if I truly trusted God. I felt like I was jumping off of a cliff into the unknown. If I were wrong, this could really hurt my family and many others, as well as myself. At this moment, all I know is that, I am suppose to jump and trust in the unseen arms of God. Here I go. Ready. One, two, three, jump!

Chapter 7

Holy Spirit Jump School

I've never jumped out of an airplane with a parachute, but I think I know what it must feel like. You come to a place where you must throw yourself into the very fears that have been trying to hold you back. Mentally, you have to make up your mind that you are going to take the risk in spite of the dangers. Fortunately, most people who parachute out of planes get some training first by attending jump school. Unfortunately, Holy Spirit jump school requires on the job training. My heart was pounding with apprehension. Suddenly, I jumped!

On Sunday I resigned the church with no plans for my future. You would think I would have felt sad. However, after I announced my resignation I felt like I was soaring in the air. All normal sense of time was lost. The excitement of knowing I was living by raw faith was a 'giant' rush, at first. The sensation of freedom was like flying through the air, defying the law of gravity. If only this moment of freedom could last longer.

At a time like this you better know and trust the people who pack your parachute. Knowing ahead of time that this day would come, God strategically placed an abundance of loyal and good people around me. They packed my spiritual, emotional, and financial parachute when I resigned. Not only did they pack my parachute for me, but they made the same leap of faith as well.

Physically, it felt like a giant mill stone was lifted off of my body. I was not aware of the tremendous weight of ministry that I had been carrying until suddenly it was lifted. I could finally take in a deep breath. I was free from the responsibility of trying to fix a broken church. Only a minister can understand this feeling that I am talking about. This personal exhilaration was short lived as I looked at the tears of many of those I would be leaving. My resignation was liberating to me but what about those who call me their pastor? Some of them felt they could no longer stay in this church if I were not there leading it. Where would they go?

This was not the way I wanted to leave my church, or end my ministry. I hoped to stay as pastor at least long enough to help them organize a pulpit committee to find another pastor. I announced my resignation would take effect in thirty days hoping this would be a way to demonstrate forgiveness and heal some wounds within this body. However this was not to be. I could see that my staying around to help prepare the way for the next pastor was not going to work like I had hoped. The moment I announced my resignation it was like the enemy was given authority to move in and take over. I soon realized it would be best that I leave as soon as possible.

This was like having a loved one die but never getting to say good bye properly. There was no closure. Suddenly the church was without a pastor and I was spiritually homeless. Even though God was the One who told me to let go, it appeared to some like I was a whipped pup and had been defeated by the opposition. I remember seeing some people smile with pure delight as I announced my resignation and almost break out in applause. It was as if they had tasted a personal victory. Their plans and strategies to remove another pastor had worked. That made me want to stay and fight to show them they were wrong, however I knew God told me to give them

> **Here I was obeying God but it looked and felt like a humiliating defeat.**

the baby and for me to jump into the unknown future. Here I was obeying God but it looked and felt like a humiliating defeat.

Every Wounded Shepherd Has Wounded Sheep

Suddenly after the thrill of jumping out of a plane, one has to face the reality that the ground is approaching faster than you realize. Even though I was the one who resigned I felt wounded, my family was wounded, and many good friends were wounded. "If this is what church is like then I wanted no part of it." I remembered making this statement to myself and to God more than once. I don't think God paid too much attention to my self pity. In fact, I thought my ministry was over. I was both glad to be free from this church mess and yet angry at the way things turned out.

When a pastor leaves a church under bad circumstances there is a ripple effect that touches many people. A wounded shepherd also means there are wounded sheep. As a result of this ugly church ordeal, a lot of people were suddenly leaving their church home with no place to go. Several were feeling the same emotions that

I was feeling; anger, disappointment, and sadness, and wondering what was next. I was free from the burden of a divided church but I was not free from caring for the people whom God called me to pastor. I may not be a pastor behind a pulpit in a church building but I was still "the pastor" to those sheep that God had assigned to me. This was not just about me, but feeling deeply disappointed with what had happened, I felt incapable of helping anyone.

The Ministerial Casualty List

Under the Levitical law no priest with a scab could enter or even be allowed to minister to anyone. A scab would indicate an unhealed wound. I was the minister with an unhealed wound and I needed ministry. My wounds were beginning to fester. Thoughts like, "Why was this happening to me? I hadn't been immoral or dishonest. I was transparent about the way God was changing me". Now at age forty six, after twenty years as a pastor, it was my turn to leave the ministry, at least this is what I thought. The feelings of failure were overwhelming. Had I wasted over twenty years of my life doing the wrong thing? Now suddenly it's over? It felt like I was reading my own ministerial obituary that sounded like this. "The ministry of Gary Washburn died when he reached the age of forty six after twenty years of faithful service. No funeral or memorial service will be provided." There was no closure.

I knew of several pastors who left the ministry and even some who had been fired for a variety of reasons. The fact is, this type of thing is happening at epidemic proportions everyday to pastors everywhere. Listen to the facts about pastors provided by maranathalife.com.

"Each month over 1500 ministers leave the ministry due to moral failure, burnout or due to division in the church. Four thousand new churches begin each year, but over seven thousand churches close. Fifty percent of pastors' marriages will end in divorce. Fifty percent of pastors are so discouraged that they would leave the ministry if they could, but they have no other way to make a living."

Just in case anyone reading this has aspirations of becoming a minister, stop and make a 'u' turn and re-read the obituary above. So many pastors end up on the walking wounded list, or worse, in the ditch of moral and family failure. You really need to count the cost. The ministry carries a heavy duty premium for the minister and the minister's family. I thought my name was now being added to the obituary list. But God had other plans.

Co-incidence or God incident?

On the evening of my resignation at the church we were at a restaurant with some of our close friends. Pam told me Terry, the worship leader I met a few months ago was having dinner on the other side of the restaurant and that I should go and say hello to him. I wasn't in any mood to talk to another minister but I did it to satisfy my wife.

Terry already heard of my resignation and sounded excited for me and said that we needed to get together and talk. He reminded me of how he felt God would have us work together some day in the future. I forced a smile while thinking to myself that I probably would never return to church ministry. Terry was very positive and persistent about getting me to agree to call him after we got back from some time away. I agreed to call him but assured him that I was not interested in anything to do with a church.

It was during this same time that Terry was feeling uneasy in the church where he also had ministered the last ten years. Tension was increasing between Terry and leadership over the freedom that he was encouraging people to express during worship. He was ordered by leadership to "tone it down". After much prayer and counseling from many people, Terry decided after ten years of service that his time at this church was over.

He called me on the phone after he turned in his letter of resignation. I was shocked to hear he was stepping down from his prestigious position as worship leader at his church. What was even more shocking was to hear how thrilled he sounded to be resigning in order to pursue his hopes and dreams of starting a non-denominational church. "Either this guy is insane or he has heard from God", I thought. He reminded me again of our first conversation where he told me that he felt one day we would be working together. I remembered that meeting and on that day I had not taken his words seriously. Now I needed to re-consider that maybe God was up to something since strangely we had both left our churches around the same time, where both of us had served the last ten years. Both of us carried a dream of starting a non-denominational church someday. Could it be coincidental that this was happening to us around the same time?

In Terry's resignation letter he wrote, "I've tasted God's manifested presence in worship and I never want to go back to limiting the work of the Holy Spirit in order to have church as usual. I have to follow my heart." His encounter with the Holy Spirit back at the worship conference had forever ruined him for 'church as usual'. I had to admit that I felt much the same way.

A backlash of support for Terry rose up when people within the church heard of his resignation. There were many who were enjoying this new freedom and style of worship at their church and wanted Terry to stay. This was not an option for Terry. He was ready to move forward toward his dream of starting a new church.

This was the end and a new beginning for Terry and others who were standing with him. This demand for freedom in worship came with a risk that Terry was willing to take. This was Terry's turn to jump into the unknown future. At some point in your faith walk you are going to have to jump! This was our turn. Yours is coming if it hasn't already! Get ready to jump.

Chapter 8

Just Start Moving!

Then the Lord said to Moses, "Why are you crying out to me? Tell the people to get moving!" Exodus 14:15

What do you do when you wake up on Sunday morning and realize you have nowhere to go? For over twenty years I was a pastor of a church and my body knew the routine of getting up early on Sunday and preparing to preach. But now my family and I were spiritually homeless. This felt so awkward. We needed some tender loving care. We needed a church family.

We visited several good churches, but still felt out of place. We were not alone in feeling this way. What about all the wonderful, supportive people who left the church when we did? These people were our spiritual family and they were spiritually homeless too. The sheep were scattered without a shepherd and this was painful to realize.

It was beginning to sink in that now someone else would pastor the people I use to pastor. Was this God's plan to scatter the sheep and give them another shepherd? I deeply cared for them and was broken hearted that many of them were saddened for me and my family. Only a few weeks ago we were all together and all seemed well. Now our whole world, as we had known it, was turned upside down. I could have never imagined such a thing as this happening to our church family. I was agonizing over all the spiritually homeless people trying to recover from an ugly church mess.

Terry kept calling me and telling me that he believed all that had happened to both of us was clearly a confirmation that God wanted us to start a new type of church in our area. I was beginning to see the possibility, but I wasn't ready to make another leap of faith so soon. I was still trying to recover from the shock of my last jump and now this guy I hardly knew, wanted me to take another leap of faith into the unknown with him? I assured myself, "He may think he has heard from God but I'm not jumping into starting a church unless I clearly hear from God for myself!"

A Life Defining Moment

Deep down I was realizing that my calling from God to be a pastor was still in me. I was still suffering from sheep bite and wallowing in some self pity. I heard it said, "You can be pitiful or powerful but you can't be both at the same time." But at this time in my life I felt pitiful and powerless.

Many "God called" pastors have walked away from ministry after church troubles to pursue a more stable lifestyle. I knew I had the freedom to make the same choice. God would not force me to stay in my calling. This was a life defining moment for me. My decision was not only affecting me but it was affecting the lives of others as well.

A decision had to be made soon. I had to have an answer to the question, "Was God calling me to start a new church with Terry?" I counseled by phone with Jack Taylor and Peter Lord, as well as many other pastors in our area, including those whom I knew would oppose the idea. The bottom line was I had to make the final decision on whether or not I was hearing from God. No one could do that for me.

I remembered the title of the sermon I preached on the day I resigned was, "God is setting you up to be blessed, if you don't mess it up." Maybe in that message I was preaching to myself more than anyone else? It was time to revisit everything that had happened to us in the last few months. Could my resignation and Terry's resignation have been somehow orchestrated by God? Was He truly setting us up to start a new church in our area? I am not saying God was the cause of the division at church. But what I am saying is what the enemy meant for evil, God would somehow use for good. Was God talking to me through all of this disappointment? How would I know for sure?

God Doesn't Guide Parked Cars

At that moment I was like a parked car not going anywhere with my life. I needed to start moving one way or the other. "God can't lead you until you start moving". I had preached that many times and now

> *God can't lead you until you start moving.*

sensed somehow that God was reminding me of my own words. "God may change your direction as you are moving but He can't change your direction if you're standing still."

Terry kept pestering me every day with a phone call wanting to know if I had heard anything from God about us starting a new church together. Each day it was becoming clearer to me that God was giving me the opportunity to start a new church with Terry. At the same time God was also giving me the free will to walk away from the ministry if that is what I really wanted.

My heart said, "It's not over until God says it's over. As much as I can discern, it ain't over!" If I was finished with ministry then my heart would not have been concerned over all the people without a pastor or a church. They could find another pastor and another church. There are plenty of good churches and pastors around this area. But somehow I knew that was not the answer.

By now Terry was chomping at the bit and each day he grew more confident that God wanted us to start a new church in the Lake or Sumter county area. He knew that I said I would not commit to anything unless I first heard from the Lord. So every day without fail he called me and asked, "Have you heard anything from the Lord yet?" Every day I dreaded telling him, "No, I still don't know anything."

It was during this time I was coming to some conclusions about what happened at our church and to our ministry. I concluded my life did not change because I resigned as pastor of a church. I was still a shepherd and the sheep that God had assigned to me were now scattered. God was not the author of the troubles in our previous church, however, God could use these troubles to get us out of where we were and to get us where we needed to be. He did not fire me from my previous church. He told me to quit! But

He never told me to quit being a pastor. I was beginning to realize He was guiding me into a new ministry!

Ready, Aim, Aim, Syndrome

I had been stalling in hopes of receiving some unmistakable voice or sign from God. In the process I became stuck in the decision making process. Decision making is much like firing a gun. Get ready, and then aim at your target and finally you must squeeze the trigger. Instead of ready, aim, and fire, I was in the ready, aim, aim, aim syndrome. I was stuck in the paralysis of analysis and was close to missing my moment of destiny. "Ready", meant for me to get ready for the next assignment. "Aim", meant I had to make a decision based on prayer and the best information that I had. "Fire", meant squeeze the trigger of decision and leave the results in God's hands. It was time to make a decision.

Believing God was leading me, I called Terry and said, "Let's start moving forward and see where God leads us." Terry was thrilled to hear this and began eagerly scouting for a place for us to have our first meeting. He had so many ideas building up inside of him that he felt as he would burst if he held onto them any longer. For me, finally making the decision was like a giant bolder rolling off my shoulders. I now had direction for my life and began moving forward again.

Naming Grace Tabernacle

What would God call this new church He was birthing? Terry met with Pam and me at our house to discuss some possible names. We all agreed it needed to have something about grace in it. The gospel is all about grace. Grace is the totally unmerited favor of God given to people who don't deserve it. At first we thought of Grace Worship Center but it just did not seem right to us. Finally Pam said, "How about using the word tabernacle because God has made His tabernacle among us by the Holy Spirit through His grace?" The combination of Grace and Tabernacle had a nice ring to it. Instantly we knew this was the name of the new church. Grace Tabernacle would be a place where people could experience the transforming power of God's grace.

Now we were facing another big issue. How do you start a church when you don't have any money or any place to meet?

Chapter 9

Our Upper Room Beginning

Once a few close friends heard of our decision to begin a new church, they offered some financial help to rent a place. So we rented an upper room in the downtown area of Leesburg, Florida. Our first Sunday meeting would be in the spring, a new season and a new beginning for all of us. Daily, the excitement was building as we moved closer to our first Sunday. It was encouraging to have enough money to rent a place, but we needed a lot more money to get the things we needed to start a church. God was about to prove He has a good sense of humor about providing for our needs.

An early morning phone call from my mom startled Pam and me awake. In a serious voice, mom said, "I've got to tell you something." Quickly, I sat up in bed, assuming it must be bad news. My mind immediately reviewed all of my relatives who might have died. She continued, "The other day, I bought a lottery ticket along with the girls at the beauty shop. I prayed over it, asking God for some money to help you start the new church. I told God that if He would let me win some money on this lottery ticket, I would give every bit of it to the church. Guess what? We won!" My jaw must have dropped to the floor. With nervous laughter, I wondered if I was dreaming.

Upon hearing this I sat up in bed stunned, and finally started laughing out loud. I was thinking, God is full of surprises. It wasn't the big lottery, but a smaller version called a Fantasy Five from which my mom had won the money. Her share of the winnings added up to approximately eighteen thousand dollars. I questioned her on giving the entire amount to the church, knowing she needed the money for herself. She insisted that God had given her the money in direct answer to her prayer. In addition to this, a couple of the other girls at the beauty shop generously gave a portion of their winnings to help start the church!

I debated over taking money from the lottery. I had even preached against the lottery and had tried to discourage my mother from playing it to no avail. I was a little uncomfortable thinking about what people would say when they heard about the source of the money. I could imagine the newspaper headlines: "Mama Won the Lotto! Helps Start New Church!" Would the church be nicknamed the 'lotto church'? Would this encourage people to pray and play?

> *"Mama Won the Lotto! Helps Start New Church!"*

Would God supply this much-needed money to help start the church through the lottery? The money came at a perfect time, but in a most uncomfortable way for me as pastor to have to explain. "Mama" winning the lotto was not what I had in mind when I was praying for some start up money for the church. God can and will answer prayers in a variety of extremely creative ways.

At one time, someone probably lost a gold coin while fishing in the water. A fish most likely came along and gulped it down, thinking it was some kind of free meal. The next thing you know, Jesus and his disciples owe some taxes. Of all things to do at this moment, Jesus mysteriously sends Peter fishing. He comes back, surprised to have caught a fish that had a gold coin in its mouth worth enough to pay all of the disciples' taxes. Now, tell me God does not have a creative sense of humor. He could have had Peter find a lost coin by the road, but instead, He had the fisherman catch a "gold fish." Our Creator is so creative about meeting our needs and at the same time to keep us full of wonder about how He will do it. This made me wonder what was going to happen next.

The First Sunday

Our first Sunday in the rented downtown upper room took place April 6th, 2003. We had no idea what to expect or how many people would show up. Our only advertising of the beginning of this new church was word of mouth. Around 10:15 a.m., my daughter Sarah came into my back room office, wide-eyed with excitement. "Do you know how many people are out there?" she asked. Without waiting for my response, she said, "This place is packed. The ushers are scrambling to find more chairs, and people are still coming in!" This was an incredible sign from God that this was indeed a work of God. Over three hundred and thirty people attended our first Sunday meeting. It was a great beginning.

However, the upper room in which we began was not a convenient place to have a church. Every Friday and Saturday, the upper room was rented for parties and wedding receptions. This meant very early every Sunday

> *It was not uncommon to have to mop up beer, vomit, or even blood ,from what could have been a saloon brawl the night before.*

morning, a crew of our people would arrive to set up sound equipment and seating for a church service. It was not uncommon to have to mop up beer, vomit, or even blood, from what could have been a saloon brawl the night before.

Some of the other tenants in the building were very upset over the noise level of the church on Sundays. It actually bothered one of the tenants so much that one day he cornered me in the back alley of our building and cursed and threatened me. He said the loud music on Sunday was ruining his business. The kids running up and down the hallways were also annoying him. I tried to apologize and said I would see what we could do to make things better. At this point, this guy was not looking for an apology. He was looking to intimidate me and run our church out of the building. He was a big guy, and I thought I was going to have to fight my way out of being cornered in the alley. Finally, after some more of his name-calling, I was able to walk away, but I was totally humiliated in front of other people. Afterwards, I was so angry I that I wished that I had fought with this guy, but I knew that would have been falling for the devil's snare.

The next day, I learned more about this irate neighbor from another tenant in the building who saw the whole unpleasant episode the day before. He told me this man was going through a divorce, was losing his business, and was sleeping in his office. On top of that, he had no automobile. I began to feel some compassion for this guy after realizing all he was going through. So I decided to stop by his office just a few doors down the hall and ask him if I could talk to him. He seemed calmer, but he was still cold toward me. He agreed to stop by my office in a few minutes.

About a month earlier, a friend gave me an old mini-van that was in good condition, but just had high mileage. I had been using it as my second car and driving it to work. Now, I realized why God had a friend give me this car. It wasn't for me. It was for me to give to this man who had become my enemy. I wasn't sure if he would take it, but it was worth a try.

A few minutes later, he knocked on my door, and I asked him to come in and sit down. Cautiously, he sat down in front of me, and I began to apologize to him about the loud church noise. I invited him to join us on Sunday morning and go back to work after church. He assured me that he was not about to do that. I couldn't change the noise level to satisfy him, but I did want him to know that I wanted to try to be a friend to him. I did tell him that I heard that he needed a car and that I had one for him if he was interested. He seemed interested, but a little suspicious.

I proceeded to tell him that there was one condition for him getting the car. He reluctantly asked what the condition was. I told him he could not buy the car, because it was not for sale. He could only have the car if he took it as a gift. He stared at me as if to say, what's the catch? I assured him the car was free and if he wanted it, he would have to receive it as a gift from me to him. From there, I proceeded to share the gospel with him, and I told him how it too was a gift that he would need to receive. He respectfully listened and agreed to take the car.

He allowed me to pray for him. I laid my hand on his shoulder and asked God to bless him with a revelation of how much He loved him. I wish I could tell you that he was gloriously saved and became a member of Grace Tabernacle, but that did not happen. He took the car and not long after that he moved out of the building. I take comfort in the fact that the gospel was shared in a way that I hope that man will never forget. Oh, by the way I did get even. I clobbered him with kindness, and it felt wonderful!

We tried to find another place so that we wouldn't make enemies of the other tenants in the building, but to no avail. Finally, we understood that this was the place God wanted us to stay for a season and resigned ourselves to the fact that we would just have to make the best of it and learn to love our difficult neighbors.

What's your plan?

People would ask me what my five-year plan or long-term plans for the church were, and I would laugh. I didn't have a five- minute plan much less a five-year plan. I am not against plans, but I don't believe any plans are worthwhile unless they come from God. I think it is wise to plan ahead, but at the same time, we must realize that only God knows the future. *"We can make our plans, but the Lord determines our steps" Proverbs 16:9.* The way this church would move into its destiny would be by staying on its knees in prayer and living in moment-by-moment dependence. It's uncomfortable not knowing where you are going sometimes. Many church people are uncomfortable with God's mysterious, and unpredictable side.

God wanted us to trust Him, decision by decision, and not get ahead of ourselves or Him. This reminds me of a scene in the movie, The Chronicles of Narnia. Near the end of the movie, one of the children asks, "Where's Aslan?" The reply reveals the mysterious side of God that we must respect and learn to trust. "You must remember, Aslan is a wild lion, and he comes and goes at will." Some churches want

> *Some churches want a domesticated Jesus that fits their theology and only does what they expect.*

a domesticated Jesus that fits their theology and only does what they expect. This was not the way it was going to be at Grace Tab. Church life would always be open to God's spontaneous leading.

Elders Added To The Leadership

As administrative issues requiring an executive decision began to weigh me down, I remembered the advice Moses received from his father-in-law. Appoint some good men around you to do things so that you will not burn out trying to do it all yourself. I began to drown in the sea of decision-making, and I knew the time had come to appoint some elders.

There were no more nominating committees or a majority vote at business meetings to determine the mind of God. Now, I had to pray, fast, and wait for God to show me His direction. This was the way He expected me to discover His will.

Before long, God clearly gave me the faces of three men. Later, the addition of the fourth completed our current team of elders. The same spirit that God placed upon me as pastor, He clearly placed upon them. This was one of the keys that enabled me to recognize who God was appointing as elders. They already had the same pastoral spirit upon them that I had. It takes one to know one. By the time I approached each man about becoming an elder, the Holy Spirit had already been working on his heart. Each one told me that they knew that God was calling them before I asked them to consider it. This was confirmation that I had heard from God. From this experience, I was learning how God would lead me as I learned to first wait upon Him. I was not to ask other people for advice before I had asked for God's wisdom and direction. I had to learn to discern the will of God for myself without depending upon listening to the opinions of others first. As long as I put God first He would lead me.

We were not prepared for the flood of youth and children that was inundating our church. Terry's wife, Kathi, had a powerful ministry to the children from day one, but we lacked provisions for the teenagers. I remembered interviewing John for the youth minister position at our previous church, and decided to contact him again. By now, John was sensing that God was about to alter his ministry too, but he was not sure how it would happen. In God's perfect timing, I called John and his wife, Christina, to set up an interview for the youth minister position at Grace Tab. It did not take long for the elders and me to realize that God was adding them to our church family. God was forming a powerful church team.

The upper room church was filling up every Sunday with new people coming from all over the region. The church's reputation was growing in the community as one where 'anything could happen'. This caused all kinds, and I do stress all kinds of people to be drawn to our church. Some bizarre things were already beginning to happen, and this was only the beginning of even more wild experiences.

Chapter 10

Let Go And Let God, If You Dare!

It was Sunday morning and the atmosphere of church suddenly changed from worship to warfare. The focus was a nineteen year old young man crying with deep sobs as he lay on his face at the altar during the beginning of the worship service. Compassion filled the room as the choir broke ranks, and then the congregation and surrounded this young man to pray. It was obvious he was in agony and something weird but spiritual was happening.

Some began to lay on their faces next to him commanding demons to leave in the name of Jesus. At the same time he began coughing and spitting up mucous on the hard wood floor. Many who had never experienced anything like this in church were wide-eyed with shock at what they were seeing. What a way to start a Sunday morning church service!

This was real and the demonic struggle that was inside this young man could be felt by everyone in the room. An all out intense deliverance session was breaking out at the beginning of church in front of everyone. As he was crying out for God's help it was as if demons were pulling him back like a tug of war. David, our deliverance minister and a guest speaker, who was also a deliverance minister took charge and were ministering to him. The two deliverance ministers were leading him to renounce every hold that Satan had on his life. Each time he renounced a stronghold, the enemy's grip would weaken in a tangible way. It was as if the young man was able to take in a deep breath and relax more each time he renounced a stronghold.

Discovering A Witch At Church

As more people crowded around him, a suspicious looking woman slowly wove her way through the crowd attempting to get close enough to try and touch the young man. From the moment she walked into the upper room, some women in our church had taken notice of her. Later, they would report that they knew something about her was not right the moment they saw her. David, our deliverance minister, felt the Lord tell him that a witch was present and that he needed to stop her.

Without hesitating, he stood up and pointed his finger at this unknown woman and spoke out in tongues with a loud commanding voice. Suddenly she stopped moving forward and a smirk came across her face as if she had been found out. Immediately, some ladies created a blockade to keep her from reaching the young man. She backed off and eventually left the building. Most of us were not aware that this lady was a witch on assignment. Through supernatural discernment, the Holy Spirit exposed the enemy and that was enough to overcome whatever he was planning to do. The young man was taken to another room for more deliverance that continued to last for several hours.

Tongues And The Interpretation

The following Thursday night was our regular meeting time for mid-week worship and prayer. I reviewed with the congregation the bizarre events that had unfolded on Sunday. While retelling the part about David speaking in tongues, someone stopped me and said, "He did not speak in tongues". "Yes he did," I said. "No, he didn't," others joined in and agreed that they had heard him speak in English. Others of us clearly heard him speak in a tongue. There were enough witnesses to verify that some heard tongues and some heard English. David clarified to us that he distinctly remembered speaking in tongues.

Some heard tongues and some heard the interpretation. It was becoming apparent that God had demonstrated a wonder before our eyes. A wonder is something that causes people to wonder at God and say, "What happened?" It felt

> *A wonder is something that causes people to wonder at God and say, "What happened?"*

as though we were re-living parts of the book of Acts as everyone continued to feel a sense of awe at the works of God among us.

More and more unusual encounters like this were happening. It was becoming quite common to hear people as they were leaving church say things like, "Wow, we have never experienced anything like this."

The Lord longs to show us what He can do when we love Him without any strings of control attached. I would often say out loud, "It's Your church, Lord. You can do whatever You want!" After I said this I often wondered why I had said it. God took my words seriously and did do whatever He wanted to do and this sometimes made me nervous. I watched very normal people display some very bizarre behaviors and I wondered if this was from God or not. Some would break out in screaming and others in laughter during the worship service. Was this a spiritual insane asylum?

So many weird and strange things were happening that Terry was seriously concerned that we were becoming known as a 'Looney' church. After one exceptionally weird deliverance session, I went away shaking my head, wondering about everything that had just happened. One of the most godly people that I knew just manifested as demons were being cast out of them. Life was becoming more bizarre by the moment. On the following day, I wrote in my journal what I felt God was saying to me.

"You are going to see many things that you do not understand but know that I am in charge. Just watch and observe. I had you there last night as an observer so that you will not doubt the greater things to come."

As the pastor, I felt that I should be able to understand the things that were happening in order to answer everyone's questions. But deep inside I felt like a child myself, and I knew that God was schooling me by giving me a front row seat in His school of the Holy Spirit.

My theological wine skin had stretched so far that I had mile long stretch marks. At one point I was concerned about our church developing a bad reputation and

"The brighter the light the greater the bugs".

becoming a weirdo magnet? You know, "The brighter the light the greater the bugs". Our light was drawing some strange bugs! Through it all, God kept sending us all kinds of hurting people. Many born again Christians who needed deliverance from demons were coming from other churches. Either their church did not believe Christians could have a demon or they did not know how to deal with them. Many were coming to Grace Tab as a last resort for help. We had to grow quickly in discernment to recognize the difference between those that really wanted help from those who just wanted attention.

God was leading us and we were rapidly learning so many new things. While nothing is new to God, most of what was happening at church was new to us. Since the beginning of Grace Tabernacle our spiritual growth chart looked something like a space shuttle launching off of the launch pad. Every week new experiences catapulted us into searching the scriptures to discover if what was happening was valid. Each day I would take long prayer walks with God and discuss these new things. I did not want to be deceived by the enemy and cross into the forbidden territory of error.

Some of the local pastors had heard of some of the things happening at our church and warned their people to stay away from us and even said that we were a cult. Some of those rumors were being spread in an attempt to keep people from visiting Grace Tabernacle. This was hurtful to hear such comments especially coming from spiritual leaders that we personally knew.

Terry was furious over hearing of some of the gossip coming from one of the local pastors and wanted to confront him. He felt justice would be served by confronting this man with his own words.

While I did not like hearing the vicious rumors either, I did not feel that we should try to defend ourselves but let God become our defender. At first Terry did not agree but submitted to my leadership anyway.

This was a test for us. If we retaliated, then we would become our own defense. This was our moment to experience grace and give grace just like Jesus.

"When they hurled their insults at Him, He did not retaliate; when He suffered He made no threats. Instead He trusted Himself to Him who judges justly."
I Peter 4:23.

Many looking for personal freedom or hungering to experience more of the power of God would secretly show up at one of our services. Terry began to understand the power of letting God be our defender. Instead of fighting back and trying to defend our reputation we ignored such negative comments realizing the works of God would validate this ministry through time. One local pastor even made the comment that we would not last six months or a year at most. Time would reveal whether that comment was true or not. Our response was not to respond to any negative comments and let God be our defender. Grace was being poured out.

To be or not to be extreme, that is the question.

From time to time, we would experience extremes that later we came to realize had more fleshly zeal than they did the Holy Spirit. In the heat of the moment it is hard to separate true passion from fleshly zeal. However, time is a great revealer of truth. The pendulum of emotion swung to the extreme on both sides. We came to realize that a church needs a healthy mix of demonstrative and reserved people. If you can help people to respect and receive one another even when they are at opposite ends of the emotional spectrum, then church becomes a place where the Holy Spirit can do a unique work. Sometimes this will require us to allow God to make us uncomfortable about some of the strange people and strange things happening around us.

The greatest problem in the church today is not immorality or drugs or any other social evil. The greatest problem facing the church today is spiritual dullness. In most church services people can predict

> **The greatest problem facing the church today is spiritual dullness.**

what is going to happen next without the use of an order of worship. Much of the church has lost its wide-eyed wonder of God and all that He can do.

Today Christians are looked upon as nice, quiet church people who you would want as your neighbors. Where are the radical followers of Christ who boldly witness and heal the sick or cast out devils, bringing the kingdom of God wherever they go? It was that way in the first century so why should it be any different today? Spiritual apathy and complacency are the greatest threats to the church today.

Even More Strange And New Experiences

"Falling under the power" was a new phenomenon to many of us. Some call this being "slain in the Spirit".

I prefer "falling under the power" because I think this more accurately describes what is happening to the individual. People can become so sensitive to the awareness of God that they literally collapse. As strange as it sounds, for some, this is a time of inner healing of some deep wounds that need God's touch. It's as if God puts them into a deep sleep before He does His surgery. Many experience an overwhelming sense of peace and comfort at this moment of yielding to the Holy Spirit. This was beginning to happen more frequently at our church and on one occasion, one of the children watching was overheard speaking to another child saying, "They're dropping like flies today!"

I was concerned about this and did not want to get caught up in emotionalism or false doctrine. I began to do some research about falling under the power of the Holy Spirit. To my surprise I began to discover this was a common occurrence during seasons of great revivals.

During the Great Awakening, this phenomenon of falling out under the power was common. At one outdoor meeting where thousands were gathering to hear John Wesley, people climbed trees to get a better view of things. They were warned to come down because it was likely that some might fall out of the trees when the power of God would manifest. A few who laughed at that idea later were observed falling with a thunk as Wesley preached.

We eventually organized several men to become catchers when this started happening frequently. I remember that a few slipped by our catchers, and I saw one lady's head bounce like a melon off the hard wood floor. To my knowledge, no one was ever injured, but I did consider issuing bike helmets to everyone at ministry time!

A Trip To Toronto

A trip to Toronto Christian Airport Fellowship helped me gain insight into what was happening at our church and what we could expect to happen. For years, I had heard of the Toronto blessing and wondered if it was true that revival had been going on there for twelve years nonstop. I knew Jack Taylor, a preacher and friend whom I trusted, had preached there, so I asked him if it was the real deal. He told me I should take a visit to Toronto and see for myself. I took four other men with me to scout this thing out. If this was a real revival where God's presence had manifested, I would know it immediately. I had to see for myself if all the stories I had heard of this place were real.

Upon arrival at the Toronto Airport Christian Fellowship sanctuary, the atmosphere was buzzing with excitement. We heard loud cries from people calling out "woe" as if they had been zapped with electricity. Other people were twitching or falling down on the floor. Others were slumped over in their chairs as if drunk. No one was touching anyone. These behaviors were just happening. During the worship, several people waved beautifully colored banners, some used tambourines and yet they all seemed oblivious to the people around them as they freely danced all over the church. People felt a great liberty to worship God without any inhibitions and everyone seemed to be getting along without any problems. It was interesting to say the least.

Our wide-eyed group from Grace Tabernacle must have been noticeable to everyone as we came into the building. We must have been gawking at all the peculiar sights and sounds. However, we were there to learn and God was stretching our wine skins so that we would be able to hold more in the days ahead.

John and Carol Arnott had heard about our church from Jack Taylor. They graciously called our group up on the stage and allowed us to share what was happening in our new church in Florida. John Arnott shared with us publicly that there had been many strange things that had happened in his church, and sometimes he had not been sure what to do about them. There will always be someone around trying to tell you what you should or should not allow in church. Turning and speaking directly to me he said, "Remember, God made you the pastor and not these other people who may try to tell you what to do. Don't try to be a Toronto; just be yourself."

I admired John Arnott's relaxed, easy going style. Even though there were thousands of people at this televised conference, he took time to speak these encouraging words to our group as if no one else was in the room. His next words

> *What you will have to learn is to pastor a revival, not police it.*

were timely words of wisdom that I will never forget. He said to me, "What you will have to learn is to pastor a revival, not police it. There will be times you are not sure if something is of God or not. You have to become sensitive to the Holy Spirit or else you might try to shut down something that is of God just because it's uncomfortable for you." These words could not have come at a better time than this when all kinds of bizarre new things were happening at out church.

Holy Laughter Liberation

On our last night of the Toronto conference, one of the members of our group and I experienced what I would call holy laughter. The strange thing is that it did not happen at the church but on the way to our hotel. We got tickled about something that happened earlier that evening and that sparked laughter that lasted for several hours. I cannot recall ever laughing so hard or so long in my lifetime. This was more than just physical laughter that was causing my side to ache and my facial muscles to hurt. It was like an aerobic workout without the treadmill. This laughter was more than the giggles. Somehow we all knew it was from God.

We literally had to stay outside the hotel and wait until the laughter subsided. We knew we could not make it through the lobby of the hotel in this condition. Surely, people seeing us would have called the police thinking we were a couple of drunks. Finally, we made it to our rooms, and I fell into a deep sleep only to awaken around three a.m. with laughter rising up in me again. This time, the Holy Spirit allowed me to stop, or else I think I would have awakened the entire hotel floor with holy laughter.

A Key to Leading the Church

I woke the next morning feeling so healthy and alive and lighthearted. Looking back, I believe that I actually experienced a physical healing during this strange experience of laughter, as well as burdens lifting. Could this have been God's way of releasing the burdens of feeling like I had to control the church?

I think God saw me becoming way too serious, and so He poured a drop of His joy medicine upon me. One drop cured me. I was instantly under the influence and was so care free that I felt like I could fly. This was a deep inner surgery where God was releasing His joy within me that would result in spiritual as well a physical healing. Even though my sides and face were in pain I knew it was supernatural medicine touching some deep hurts inside me. I could not explain it, I just knew it.

"A merry heart doeth good like a medicine." Proverbs 17:22.

Learn to Discern

A few years later a prophet came to me with a strong word that I realized was from the Lord. This word was a warning to me. "Don't give away your discernment. You must not give away your discernment by letting others tell you the mind of the Lord. You must discern for yourself what I want you to do."

> **Don't give away your discernment!**

Without realizing it, I was trusting others with special giftings of discernment rather than trusting the Holy Spirit to lead me as the pastor. This was a corrective word from God to me that I needed at this particular time in order to lead our church.

I've never forgotten this. There have been times where I could have been intimidated by someone's charisma or obvious spiritual gift of discernment. But then I would remember the word from the prophet and would realize that I had to make all final decisions for the church from the discernment that God was giving me. This would not be easy, especially when sometimes my final decision may oppose other leaders' opinions in the church. But God was making it clear to me that He made me the pastor and the buck stops with what God reveals to me. If I am wrong then I can trust God to correct me.

This leadership style was not one that came naturally to me. All my previous pastoral experience was under the congregational government style where the people voted on decisions concerning the church. Now I had to know the mind of God concerning a matter before I listened to the advice of other people.

Trusting the Great Shepherd to lead me to shepherd this new kind of church would be a challenge for me for the rest of my life. I do not have to understand it all, neither do I have to explain it all. My part is to trust that God knows how to communicate to me and to lead me to be the pastor. The people would have to trust that God was leading me as I was leading them. Risky? Certainly, but at the same time a necessary part of our walk of faith. The call of God was clear to me now. Let go and let God, if you dare. I surrendered my false burden of feeling I had to be in control. This was a necessary part of our church transitioning toward the exciting next level.

Chapter 11

The Transition For Position

For over two years, Grace Tabernacle met in the crowded upper room in downtown Leesburg. From the Upper Room, we moved into a warehouse that was transformed into a sanctuary and allowed us room to grow. We became known as the 'Warehouse Church'. The power of God which we had experienced in the downtown Upper Room continued in even greater measure at the Warehouse.

Long before I ever came to Leesburg, I had read about the great revival that happened at a local Baptist church back in the seventies. Some of the people in our church had been a part of that great outpouring. They frequently commented that what we were experiencing at Grace Tab, was similar to the revival they had experienced during the seventies at Westside Baptist.

I was curious and wanted to find out more. Pastor Dick Coleman was pastor of the Westside Baptist Church during this revival. By now he had passed away, but his wife, Minnie, was leading a retreat ministry called Living Waters in North Carolina. Some friends in our church gave me her phone number, so I called her. Instantly, during our phone conversation, I felt the need to meet Minnie in person. Somehow, I knew this was a kingdom connection for us. Consequently, I invited her to preach at our church.

She came to our Warehouse Church on a Sunday night and preached from Genesis 26. The scripture was about Isaac re-digging his father's wells that the Philistines had covered. Minnie continued to speak about the time the Holy Spirit touched down in her Baptist church and a revival began that drew curious people from all over the world. This revival continued several years and brought well-known Bible teachers like Derek Prince, Bob Mumford, Kenneth Hagin, and many others to little Leesburg.

During her preaching, Minnie hesitated for a moment as if she were weighing her words carefully before she spoke. After a long pause, she said, "I believe God is re-digging those wells today that were dug during the revival in Leesburg and He is passing on the same anointing we had onto Grace Tabernacle. I believe I have the authority from God to pass this anointing that was given to my generation to Grace Tabernacle, and this is why I am here." I was stunned but excited that this seasoned saint, who had experienced revival first-hand, believed God was leading her to pass the torch on to us, much like the Olympic torch is passed on. Could the fire of revival be passed on to us to carry? How would I know if this was really happening?

Visible Confirmation

After delivering the brief message, Minnie, in her simple grandmotherly style, began to minister by praying and laying hands on people who came forward for ministry. The power of God mightily touched down among us as if God were saying a visible 'amen' to the message just delivered. People were falling under the power of God as Minnie laid hands on them. It was holy chaos as bodies were laying all over that warehouse floor. The catchers could not keep up with the people falling.

The power of God in the atmosphere was so tangible that no one wanted to leave. People continued to line up, waiting to experience this special touch from God. That night, church continued until almost one o'clock in the morning! God was confirming that He was redigging the wells and He had chosen Grace Tabernacle to carry the torch of revival.

The Vision Of The Cow Pasture

The Warehouse Church was a rented facility and we knew we would soon have to move again. Where did God want Grace Tabernacle to be located? A lady in our church shared a vision in which she saw our new church building in the middle of a cow pasture. When I heard this, I thought to myself, "Oh great! Just what we need! To be out in the middle of nowhere, known as the cow patty church."

Not long after this, a man who had not heard about this vision, donated five acres of his cow pasture to our church. By this time, we had the money to purchase another six acres from an adjoining property. The vision of the cow patty church was coming to pass after all.

From an Upper Room to a Warehouse and now a cow pasture but we still needed a building. After a lengthy process, a loan was secured, the building was built, and we moved from the warehouse to the current building of Grace Tabernacle in December 2006. Our first worship service in the new building was on Christmas Eve. It was as if God was saying, "Here's an early Christmas gift for you."

On December 31, we also had the first wedding in our new building. Our church administrator, Jenni, and her husband, Brian, were the first to be married in our new sanctuary. The circumstances surrounding this marriage made it not only unique but also prophetic to our church. Their purity and willingness to wait upon the Lord for the right mate and the right time was a testimony to all of us about waiting upon God and trusting His timing. It was as if God was saying to Grace Tab, "Now you are in the right place and now it is the right time. Grace will be multiplied and spread to the whole world."

An Unforgettable Dream

In May of 2007, I had a dream that I was playing football on a football field. The ball was kicked to our team. A player behind me tried to catch the ball but it bounced out of his hands back up into the air and landed perfectly into my hands. This is too easy, I thought. Now running with the ball, I zigzagged around several of the other team's players with little effort, thinking to myself, this is such unusual favor.

I asked the Lord what this vivid dream meant, and this is what He revealed to me: "You are no longer on the defense but on the offense.

> *You are no longer on the defense but on the offense.*

I have strategically placed you where you are in life to lead my team. The earth is the playing field and your team is my church.

The problem is that my team has forgotten that there is a time limit to their game. They only have a small amount of time left to score and achieve My goal. Time is my gift to you. But what you do with it is your gift back to me.

This should make us all think about how we are spending our lives and calculate how much time we may have left in the game.

If you are:	This means you have:
20 years old	2,500 weekends left
30 years old	2,000 weekends left
40 years old	1,500 weekends left
50 years old	1,000 weekends left
60 years old	500 weekends left" [1]

In my dream, the ball first came to someone else but then bounced out of his hands and fell into mine. This is exactly how I felt when I first became the pastor of Grace Tabernacle. It's humbling to think that I may not have been God's first choice to run with the ball. Maybe He gave the opportunity to someone else and for whatever reason, they fumbled it and it was divinely dropped into my hands. This is scary when I think how close I had been to quitting the ministry. Everyone has a God assignment for their life. As long as you don't quit, you will win.

During the month of January, 2006 we had a special church event called "Breakthrough to Freedom" to celebrate our grand opening of our new church building. At this event we hosted well known ministries like John Bevere, Karen Wheaton and Jason Upton that drew a large crowd of people from all over the State. An older couple who had seen our advertisement attended the conference. The moment they saw the property and the new building, they burst into tears realizing that they had seen this property years ago. After they gained their composure, they told one of our ushers that over ten years ago they had driven by our property when the Spirit of the Lord whispered to them that they were to start a church here.

Ten years had gone by, and they had forgotten that special moment until they had driven onto the church property. It was as if God was showing them what He would have done if they had obeyed His voice. Maybe they were God's first choice, and since they did not seize this opportunity, God ordained the ball to fall into my unassuming hands, as if to say, "It's your turn. Run with it!"

1. Evidence Bible

Chapter 12

Upward And Onward To The Next Level

As I am writing this last chapter, I am sitting in a Florida beach penthouse that some gracious people in our church allowed us to use for a much needed vacation. This isn't just any beach condo. This is a private luxurious penthouse in an exclusive area. We have never been here before and so we did not know what to expect. We were told by the owners to expect to be impressed. That proved to be an understatement!

As we drove into a beautifully landscaped driveway, we slowly edged up to the gated guardhouse, wondering if we were in the right place. Our older model car was probably a giveaway that we didn't belong here. The guard was expecting us or else he might have turned us away. We drove through the gate into what looked like a Garden of Eden landscape. We drove around the tennis court and into a garage that led us to another private garage that was inside. From there, we stepped out of our car into a hallway with a private elevator that took us and all our luggage, including Wal-Mart bags to the penthouse.

As the elevator opened into a private foyer, our jaws dropped onto the marble floors as we peered at the double doors leading into the palatial penthouse. We arrived in Donald Trump-Ville! My wife and I looked at each other with the look the Beverly Hillbillies had when they first stepped inside the mansion. We have never experienced luxury like this in our lifetime. Not only was the beach view stunning, but the interior of this penthouse was captivating as well. Quickly, we traveled from room to room, gawking at bedrooms and bathrooms that could easily be on the television show "Lifestyles of the Rich and Famous."

The next morning, we awoke to the sound of ocean waves as the sunlight peeked over our balcony, gradually lighting the bedroom. As I opened my eyes, my first thoughts were, I have died and this is heaven! A few moments later, we sat at the glass breakfast table with Bibles open and sipping morning coffee while waiting for the caffeine to kick in. Glancing up from reading, the sight of the ocean mesmerized our attention. As if in a hypnotic trance, we gazed into what looked like a billion diamond-shaped crystals reflecting the morning sun. I heard in my thoughts, *"Be still and know that I am God" (Psalm 46:10)*.

I thought to myself, I need to slow down and pay more attention to all of the wonder of God's creation around me that I so often take for granted. Staring into the ocean, I wondered why I don't wonder more often. Creation is filled with wonders, and they should drive us to want to know the God of wonder.

> **I wondered why people don't wonder more at God's creation?**

In a place like this, I thought how easy it would be for me to become a sage, a philosopher, a man who thinks deeply about God and life, things most people never have the time to think about. The sights and sounds of the beach were tranquilizing. At that moment, my deepest thought was, Life is good in the penthouse. I could get used to this. I became bold and asked God if I could live here in the penthouse for the rest of my life. I think I heard Him laugh. I took that as a no. Then in my mind it was as if God were saying, "My dear child, I have so much more for you than this. There is so much more of Me for you to experience. Things that will thrill your soul and cause you to wonder all through eternity." I sat there stunned at the thoughts that I just heard.

Suddenly, overwhelmed by the luxury inside this penthouse as well as the glory of creation outside, I started to wonder some more. Why am I here sitting in this luxurious penthouse on a beautiful beach? Is this just a kind, gracious act of some compassionate people or has God ordered this luxurious week of vacation to show us something? The answers are yes and yes.

Imagine, all of your life, you have struggled just to get by and pay the bills. For most of us, imagination isn't required for this exercise. Stay with me and keep imagining. Suddenly, you just inherited billions of dollars from a distant relative. Overnight, you are wealthy beyond your wildest imagination. A person who owes you

> *You can't learn this revelation by reading a book, it must come through experience.*

money contacts you. Unaware of your recent inheritance. He shows up at your door and begins to apologize for not having the full amount that he was to pay you by today. You can see that he is embarrassed as he asks you to grant him a little more time. You are so overwhelmed with your good fortune that you quickly tell this friend,

"Forget about it; you don't owe me a thing. In fact what else do you need that I can help you with?" This guy is shocked by the grace with which you have treated him and walks away scratching his head and thanking God.

Wouldn't it would be natural for you to be so gracious, because, you have received an abundance of grace yourself? Within our spiritual bank account, a huge deposit of grace has been made by our Heavenly Father. It is an over payment of the loving kindness of the Lord, that we call grace. The fact that God loves us so much that He would give His only Son for us is incomprehensible. However, you can't learn about this grace by reading a book, it can only come through experience. There is no other way.

God will arrange divine opportunities for us to personally discover how extravagant His love is towards us. These divine opportunities often come in surprise packages that don't look so divine at first.

Some of the bitter disappointments we will encounter in this life with people and circumstances are nothing more than divine tests; designed to build the endurance necessary for us to reach our destiny.

God knows what it takes to get us to the next level of faith. He knows we need endurance to be able to reach our destiny. Endurance training requires deliberate exercises done over and over again to increase stamina and muscle strength. Did you catch the part about over and over again?

Many times God will cross our path with people who disagree with us over some issue. We may see this as an obstacle; but God sees this as an opportunity to build endurance in our love. Choosing to love is an act of yielding our circumstances to a loving God who has our best interest in mind. As we yield, He is able to demonstrate a sermon to a world that desperately needs to see a sermon rather than hear another one. This choice to yield to God allows Him to step into any situation and make something good come out of something bad.

Early in my ministry, I had several disagreements with a deacon in the church. Every time I turned around, it was as if I was butting heads with this guy. I was so fed up with him that I had decided that I was going to set him straight. A few days later, a prophet that I did not know showed up at my office unexpectedly and said he had a word from God for me. Curiously I listened to what he had to say. He said, "You have been having some trouble with a man in your church. Be gentle with him because he is a

> *I became aware that God was in this difficult situation that I was trying to escape.*

brother in the Lord." He prayed for me; then he left and I never saw him again. That experience stopped me in my tracks. God saw me in my frustration and what I was about to do and warned me to walk in love and grace. My whole attitude changed and eventually this man became a dear friend and was a great help to me in the church. What made the difference? First, I became aware that God was in this difficult situation that I was trying to escape. Second, God was using it to show me what His supernatural love and grace would do if I allowed Him to flow through me. Part of the solution was for me to see how much God loved this man which made it easier for me to love him. When the love of God was allowed to flow in me then it became easy to allow the love of God to flow through me.

Some of the greatest obstacles to overcome in our Christian maturity will be from brothers and sisters in the church. Brothers in the Lord don't always get along. Genesis records how the half brothers of Joseph were extremely cruel to him, but love wrote a surprising last chapter to that story. Joseph knew that God had more for him and that he would not be in prison for the rest of his life. The dreams God had given him would somehow come true. At

> **The greatest obstacles to overcome in our Christian maturity will be from brothers and sisters in the church.**

the right time God promoted Joseph from the prison to the penthouse overnight. He was positioned to have the upper hand over his brothers. Now what would he do?

Even when Joseph had the opportunity to get revenge, he resisted and showed great grace. He knew the world's way of getting justice was not God's way. Because his brothers sold him into slavery, he spent eleven years of his life as a house slave, and then two more years in prison. He had every right to be consumed with anger and hatred towards them. In the end, he found grace to stand before his brothers without an ounce of bitterness toward them and say, *"You meant it for evil, but God meant it for good"* *Genesis 50:20.*

It was never God's desire for Joseph to experience all of the heartache that he had in his life. God always meant good things for Joseph. Only because Joseph had the true revelation of God was he able to respond to his brothers in the same way that Jesus would have. Passing this test, God promoted Joseph to the next level in his life. It works the same for you and me.

If you find yourself angry, hurt, or disappointed by someone, then you naturally want justice. Don't go after justice for yourself or for anyone else. If you settle for getting justice with your enemies, you are settling for less than you should. God is a god of justice.

If someone wrongs you and you take matters into your own hands to settle the score, then that will be all of the justice that you will get. When the scales are balanced, there is justice. As long as you attempt to bring justice to a situation, you are forcing God to remove His hand from the matter. This is your opportunity to experience God's grace like never before.

"This is the kind of life you've been invited into, the kind of life Christ lived. He suffered everything that came His way so you would know that it could be done, and also know how to do it, step-by-step"

I Peter 2:21 Message.

One thing the devil has not seemed to realize yet is God is always way ahead of all of the moves that he makes. Every trial in our Christian life has a divine opportunity hidden inside. Some trials God deems as necessary for us

> *Every trial in our Christian life has a divine opportunity hidden inside.*

to endure. Unfortunately for us, we don't get to decide which ones are necessary or not.

*"In this you greatly rejoice, even though now for a little while, **if necessary**, you have been distressed by various trials"* (*I Peter 1:6*).

At the time of this writing it has been almost seven years since the beginning of Grace Tabernacle. We have experienced mountain peeks of glory, as well as discouraging times where I felt like quitting. The ride has been exhilarating and somehow I feel that we are on the verge of breaking through a barrier that few have ever experienced! I tremble as I consider how the enemy will do anything within his power to get us to back down. I know there will be more tests.

In 1947, Chuck Yeager became the first American pilot to break the sound barrier in the X-S-1 aircraft. The 'X' stood for experimental. The 'S' meant it would fly at supersonic speed, and '1' indicated this would be the first aircraft to break the sound barrier. Yeager determined to be the first American to do it, or die trying.

Many skeptics said that this was crossing a forbidden boundary. It was stepping into the unknown and there was a lot of speculation as to what might happen. Would the pilot black out from the pressure of the G-forces on his body? Would the plane collapse under the extreme pressure? There was only one way to find out.

From subsonic to supersonic speed, there is a wind build up on the nose and wings of a plane that cause it to shake violently. It is at this moment, the pilot either backs off, fearing the plane may fall apart, or he pushes ahead into the unknown.

Many Christians reach the point of a spiritual breakthrough, but when the shaking begins, they back off, and drift back to what is considered by some to be, "normal Christianity."

Yeager reached the barrier and made the decision to throttle up and push through. After accelerating he lost complete control of the plane, just for a few seconds. The pressure shook the plane to the point of nearly breaking apart. At that moment, all of the forces pressuring the front of the plane moved to the back, thrusting the plane forward and breaking through the sound barrier.

The very thing resisting your progress eventually becomes the thing that propels you forward to breaking through the barrier. The sonic boom you hear is an announce-

> *The very thing resisting your progress... propels you forward into your break through.*

ment that you have just broken through a barrier that few will ever do. [1]

Our spiritual ride is still upward to the next level, sometimes with a whole lot of shaking going on. Maybe you read this book because you are hungry for more of the Christian life than you have experienced. Your hunger is a good sign that God has more for you. When you truly follow the Holy Spirit, strangely you may encounter some Christian people who try to discourage you from seeking more. Some will say you are extreme and going too far. Others may even tell you that you are crossing forbidden boundaries. When you hear those words, consider it your sonic boom announcing your breakthrough into the supernatural life that you were created for. You knew there was more for you. This is only the beginning. There is more!

Footnote:
1.Sermon excerpt from Larry Randolph.

How To Order

Send check or money orders to:

Grace Tabernacle
7279 E County Rd 468
Wildwood, FL 34785
(352) 748-3255
www.gracetab.org

Made in the USA
Middletown, DE
22 February 2022

61628379R00066